$F U N E S$

(Foo nez)

In dedication to my nephews,
Kavyion Antonio Hicks and Gavin Michael Nelms.

FUNES

```
F
R        Y
E        O        I
E
      F  U  N  E  S
A    R    T    V    E
L    S    O    E    R
L    E         R    E
     L         L    N
     F         A    I
               S    T
               T    Y
               I
               N
               G
```

STEVEN A. FUNES

Library of Congress Control Number:		2010906052
ISBN:	Hardcover	978-1-4500-9258-6
	Softcover	978-1-4500-9257-9
	Ebook	978-1-4500-9259-3

This book was printed in the United States of America.

To order additional copies of this book, contact:
Xlibris Corporation
1-888-795-4274
www.Xlibris.com
Orders@Xlibris.com
78274

Contents

Chance of Birth

When expressing the wonderful occasion of a birthday,
You're speechless as you can't find the right words to say.
Imagine a day where you felt reborn,
Instead of feeling old, broken away and torn.
To some, their birthday is nothing out of the ordinary.
To others, it's a radiant free spirit to carry.
Many people take their birthdays for granted,
As they wish for rebirth when their lives become slanted.
Some people actually enjoy this opportunity;
Obtaining another chance to create a new "me."

This sort of resembles a new year's resolution,
As it marks a year's end into memory conversation.
On a day such as this, one has a choice to make,
But most do not realize what's really at stake.
Almost all make the choice of the brainwashed tradition,
That is to think of oneself, forgetting all others in relation.
Quite miraculous once you understand the human mind,
As the seemingly unselfish try to hide their selfish bind.
Perfectly natural for us to think of oneself,
But all must realize what's on the top shelf.
This shelf contains the most important ideal ever;
That this world we know does not revolve around you forever.
In fact, the world does not revolve around you in the least bit,
So take your egocentric selfishness and reveal the culprit.
When your birthday comes around just remember one thing,
Solely what you choose to give, not what the world decides to bring.

Reality

Every day of your life, a pattern continues;
The pattern of the good and bad habits that you use.
From paying our bills on time to driving recklessly,
Our habits reflect our individuality.
One daily habit that people struggle with most
Is not thinking once about the powerful Holy Ghost.
There is ignorance in thinking that man created all,
For God has established this earthly rotating ball.
Yet many people continue to live without Him,
As their minds become fogged from miscellaneous whim.

People tend to set a priority on obtaining a lot of "stuff,"
As they buy and buy because what they have is not enough.
As people become misguided in these materialistic things,
They all seem to forget what God's love brings.
We say that we're busy, we go on Sunday and that's it,
But God wants full custody, not just weekend visits.
We're so selfish of our time that we constantly make excuses,
But in a fight between God and oneself, guess who loses?
Quite funny how our passions ignite with our interests,
From our sports and hobbies to the rest of our business.
But when you're asked about church or whether you are a Christian,
Quite comical how your face displays half of the passion.
The human race needs to get their act together and realize
That they don't want to get to judgment day and be caught by surprise.
So there's a message to be said by all gentlemen and divas,
'You can have the whole world! Just give me Jesus!'

Into The Deep

Birth, life, death; is that all there is to it?
Many people think so, but there's much more than what is lit.
People take life for granted as if guaranteed another.
When we say 'Live life to the fullest,' we surely don't mean to stutter.
When discussing life's potential, that doesn't mean to live carelessly;
Simply signifies contributions to the world in its reality.
Life is surely not just something for you to enjoy;
Primarily life is for you to bring others happiness and joy.
What better place to start than deep and within,

The depth of family is certainly where to begin.

Most have the influence of a mother and a father;

Some are less fortunate and do not have either.

Nonetheless, we all choose someone to love,

Whether a sibling, or a friend or the Man up above.

In any family, we learn the toughest skills of survival,

Including the emotional, mental and spiritual revival.

The love-hate aspect can become very intense,

But that gets rid of surprises, thus eliminating suspense.

The power of family is a very powerful force;

This teamwork can bypass any obstacle course.

As one gets older, they sometimes seem to lose track

Of their family, but sometimes they just refuse to look back.

They continue their lives convinced that all is well,

But day by day, their grudge continues to swell.

No matter what occurred, you should find time to forgive,

Before time escapes you and you have nothing else to give.

You can certainly aid others; that is the goal in life,

But you cannot do much if you haven't cleansed your own knife.

Life's Dealer

Millions awake and stare into the mirror,

As they hope for life's answers to become much clearer.

These millions I speak of inhabit multiple differences,

From physical, emotional or circumstantial inferences.

Day by day, we carry out our lives,

Mobilized in routine while ignoring our vibes.

From an outside perspective, we're not very far apart;

After all, we're all humans containing a mind and a heart.

But we all enter this world in a different situation;

With a silver spoon, or in a totally different equation.

When sitting with the dealer, you're dealt a hand face down,

But in life you get to decide the royal figures who wear the crown.

In life, like the game, you can't choose the cards you get,

But play your hand well and in life, you'll be set.

So ladies and gentlemen, wake up your senses;

Smell the fresh air, touch the red roses.

Taste the passion, and hear your own voices.

See more of what you can be, not of what you cannot become;

You may think your life is the worst, but yours is a lot better than some.

So relax for a moment and focus on the bright side,

Thanks to your faith in God, you are still alive.

Dreaming With Passion

Always fun to reminisce in the great memories of our past,
Trying to collect all we can remember and savoring to make them last.
As a child, our imagination begins, as we develop hopes and dreams,
And through our smaller fields of vision, the world is not what it seems.
In our childhood minds, we knew what we wanted to be;
A singer, dancer, sports athlete and many others among popularity.
As we grow older, our mind and body slowly begin to change,
As our lives begin to fall into a smaller reality range.
So we live our lives with our new interests and claim to be satisfied;

Either your life is filled with spontaneous passion
or is considered just a routine glide.
Many have lost sight of or have never really known the true purpose of living;
This purpose is one of destiny that you are currently choosing.
You always have a choice, so try to make the right decision.
Think positively with accuracy and select with high precision.
'What do I do now?' is a question that all must face,
Especially as we get older, for we begin to run out of space.
Many are in frustration with the careers they are amid,
As they have lost sight of their dreams that they had when they were a kid.
If this shoe is just your size, there's something to consider;
Think of something you really enjoy doing and use this to reconsider.
'What would you do for nothing?' is the question of consideration;
That is, what would you do as a hobby or career without money in the situation?
Answer this and you will replace the old you, who was faithless;
Ignore this and you will discover a life with no purpose.
Continue with your excuses and life will never become clear;
This will only fog your windshield and create your strongest fear.

Enemies In The Mirror

'I had a dream . . . ' yes, that sounds familiar to many;
Life filled with dreams, yet nightmares a plenty.
The scariest moment that all feared from the start,
Is people existing together yet living so far apart.
Surely we come in contact with one another every day,
But certainly life wasn't always as peaceful as today.
Blacks and whites clashing, wars all over the world;

Judging the deaf and blind, discrimination swirled.

Some believe in a god, and others believe in none;

Someone holding a cross results in another pointing a gun.

The passion of disagreement, like two magnets repelling;

The fighting and the hatred just continued swelling.

But all of that is old news, with Obama becoming our President;

That awful world from the past where one is now no longer a resident.

Many thoughts still don't quite correlate with these;

Surely things have improved, but there's still an unwanted breeze.

Why do humans still fight against one another?

Why can't everyone see that we're all one's sister and brother?

Why is there bitterness just because of our differences?

A brief moment of peace, war in all other instances.

Personal culture makes us unique, not one's enemy;

One can't compare their beauty to another's deformity.

What if you were of a different race, couldn't hear or couldn't see?

What if you looked different and beautiful you thought you could never be?

No one chooses to live with things such as this;

Everyone longs to live in a peaceful bliss.

No one person is the same, so don't stare;

Those you perceive as different don't appreciate your evil glare.

Unity may be a bit of a stretch for mankind,

But why would one want to live with such a hateful bind?

Imagine the world pitch black, and then try to visualize;

Quite comical how one would then perceive the world without eyes.

Everyone has more to offer the world than what meets the eye,

So stop pulling each other down; instead, push one another towards the sky.

As Far As The Eyes Can Feel

Letting your day go away, as you conclude another page in love;
Falling asleep in the arms of your mate, as both are dreaming in the clouds above.
Holding hands through all that occurs, jumping through all hoops together;
Being each other's backbone, joined at the hips, despite all stormy weather.
Preserving the moments of happiness, no matter how often they come;
Living the dream of finding love, something that is rare to some.
Coming home with great anticipation, much love to give and words to say;
Surprising you as she glares out the window,
looking through rain on a sunny day.

Crying with misunderstanding, as the emotions trickle down her face;

Tugging at your heart, the love slowly unravels like a shoelace.

Dating back to the very beginning, where truth collided with sin;

Losing sight of significant memories, just when did the past begin?

Enjoying the vast connection, the feeling of opposite flesh;

Grinding the pair of souls to music, so clean and so fresh.

Defining the meaning of love between the two, searching for what else to do;

Losing one's love on a single thing that the person won't do for you.

Loving a person so much, not wanting to see them cry once more;

Sacrificing your life for their own happiness, just letting them exit the door.

Choosing the right decision, just when will the future end?

Keeping the love bond tight, paving your souls around the endless bend.

Professional Soldier

Four-thirty in the morning, alarm clock ringing;
Military life, what shall this lifestyle bring me?
Left all I knew behind, happy tears soaked in my shoulder;
Moving forward in training to become a professional soldier.
Experiencing wild things, extravagance up and down my path;
Countering life's frustration as if travelling in a bubble bath.
Completing every objective possible, yet still asking why?
Why do I still feel that something has passed me by?

Assured every single day that soon will arrive my turn,
To survive in the battle zone and watch the enemy burn.
Aside from my career, I am young becoming a man;
Making a difference, utilizing all my lifespan.
Travelling through the airport, on my way home,
In my uniform, no one around me feels alone.
'I appreciate all you've done,' 'Thank-you for your service,'
Such hospitality, like a warm hug and a soothing kiss.
My home away from home was as interesting as can be;
My true home is priceless, as I now have my family.
No matter where my journey takes me, no matter which way I turn,
There is no need to worry, your soldier will always return.

So Bitter, So Sweet

Inhaling what is considered your life-long habit,
Exhaling your troubles along with smoke from your cigarette.
Allowing something to become a part of your life,
Yet continuing to be stabbed by this inevitable knife.
If the fact that your family comes first is true,
Then why has this habit gotten the best of you?
Your husband, your children and grandson are here with you,
Yet the cigarette in your mouth receives more of your time than we do.

We understand that you acquired this habit as a little girl,

But you have thrown your own life into this timeless swirl.

You are much grown up now, yet your habit is still young;

What if your outer beauty was as smoke-infested as your lung?

You can bet that you would quit if your life depended on it,

But your life actually does, so why haven't you done it?

What is your ultimate reason as to why you have given up?

You have yet to quit smoking and have in a sense, quit on us.

What about the grandchildren that you will have from me by your side?

What about your loving husband, who, if you were gone, would be dead inside?

We love and appreciate you, so don't take advantage,

Your name inscribed on our hearts, covered in permanent bandage.

Unconditional Yet Understood

Awakening to bright lights, loud sounds and such;
Arriving into a new world can surely be a bit much.
Falling into the arms of the one who made you,
Glistening into the eyes of who made your life come true.
This unconditional love depicted here is priceless;
The inevitable adoration is in every hug and every kiss.
From the very first day to our very future's end,
There lies a unique parent/friendship blend.
Certainly the mommy has to be a mother first,

Supplying all your needs: discipline, hunger, thirst;
The very discipline that creates the man or woman you need to be,
The hunger for what's further than our own eyes can see.
The thirst for success and a life you won't regret;
This blend is as remarkable as a tropical sunset.
At a point she has taught you just about all she can teach;
So, so proud her chest is as far out as she can reach.
Coming to you for advice, some support or just someone to talk to,
Being there every time and always saying, 'I'm here for you.'
Although she is the mom, sometimes she looks up to you,
Admiring the person you've become and see you as her best friend too.
Loving every aspect of you because it is her seed that grew,
Enjoys watching you grow and is proud of everything that you do.
Letting her baby go is the toughest task of motherhood,
But in the midst of all emotions, in the end, it's all good.

Underestimating Your True Identity

Skydiving, buying a new car, fun-filled vacations,

Giving into life's very own morally-sound temptations.

Asking questions like 'Should I?' 'What if?' 'Maybe?'

Willing to step outside the box and create your own reality.

Many people misguide their lives by the examples set before them,

Attempting to grow bountiful leaves with an imaginary stem.

Fear of the unknown, wondering where the journey runs;

Dare to ask the right questions or refuse to answer the wrong ones.

Waking up and stepping into the same footsteps everyday;

Never stepping out of routine to explore what the world has to say.
As a child we adore nearly all of the above,
Unfortunately the older you get, the fewer things you love.
Illustrating the simple fact that there is more to life than you may think,
Yet we slowly fade out our childhood passion and in our minds, we sink.
We must ignore what we think is true and pay attention
to what we're unsure of,
The most complex obstacles can be absolved with happiness and love.
So what if you're not a millionaire with nice cars and a large estate,
You must begin to accept the riches that you already have at stake.
Who defines the idea of rich, beautiful or happiness?
Why let society blindfold you from your own life and all the rest?
Guidelines on how to live have been passed down through each generation,
With living your own life, there is no rule book in any nation.
So has society misguided you, or have you just failed to pay attention?
Are you living just because you're alive, or is there something else
you forgot to mention?
Death is part of the cycle within each and every one of us,
Go against all odds; don't underestimate your own trust.
So enjoy your family and friends and don't let the simple things pass you by,
Because inevitably the truth makes everything else seem like a lie.

Hope, Faith and Charity

Peering through the blinds, awaiting the sun rising,

Watching your entire life crawl to the horizon,

Taking life one day at a time, as many emotions arise,

With all of them combined, you soon become hypnotized.

Happy that you have it all, and have no need to yearn for more,

Sad that you haven't found anything you want to live for.

Stressed over the gaps of distance away and time apart,

Relieved that you made it this far without anyone to break your heart.

Upset that there comes a time when many things don't go your way,

Understanding that there is much work to be done before you play.

Surprised that the smallest things become most important to you,

Ashamed in taking for granted the many lies that were true.

Sincere with the relationships between one's family and one's friend,

Excited at the possibility that good times don't have to end.

These emotions are internalized, yet they seep through the cracks,

Resulting in body language, portraying the voice that speech lacks.

Until death do us part, love always resides,

Along with the inevitable emotions at your sides.

Sometimes you find yourself wondering what to do next,

'IDK . . . LOL' says your life through a text.

You may think that one's love is physically untraceable,

But the bond that one has with their soul mate is unbreakable.

Opening all windows and doors to shine sunlight through your life,

Expanding opportunities to meet your everlasting wife.

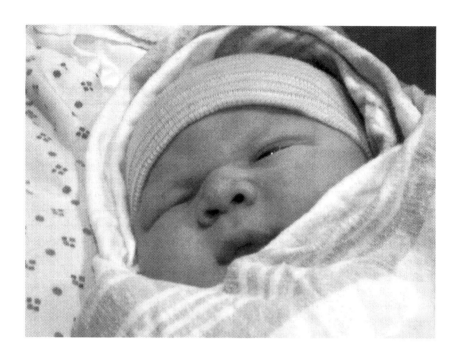

Once A Child, Always Apparent

Walking around in an endless maze, subtle fear in their eyes,

Searching for a sense of direction, receiving minimal truth and countless lies.

To some of you this reference just may apply to you,

For some this may be true, but for many they haven't a clue.

The problem with this is that adults think their life is bad,

But you were a child once right? Days were happy, some were sad.

The new era we live in, one filled with technology,

Problems of every aspect of life in society.

You think times are tough, with all this modern warfare,

Try putting yourself in the shoes of your very own childcare.

The care for your child, your children in your keeping,

Providing them with just the minimum, ignoring their weeping.
Your child's weeping for more of your time and your love in their life,
Yet you wonder why they wonder about that gun or that knife.
The way they see the world is entirely up to you,
There's a foundation under their feet that's created with everything you do.
What you say and how you say it, what you do and how you do it,
Every day they use their senses and record every single bit.
Your child wants to be just like you, they see you as their hero,
Looking at you as if watching a superhero TV show.
A positive influence from you creates a positive life for them,
Yet to this day the exact opposite happens time and time again.
Surely other influences are in this world that we've created,
You're not their only impact, but you've already seen that previously stated.
So why would you think it's okay for your child to live without you?
Why would you falsely convince yourself that everything you say is true?
The children are the ones in the timeless maze, their souls stricken with fears,
Aren't you tired of seeing their hearts bleeding with your tears?